God's Master Plan
for Women in Marriage

God's *Master Plan for* Women *in Marriage*

Heather Jean Wilson Torosyan

COMMUNITY CHRISTIAN MINISTRIES
MOSCOW, IDAHO

Read more from the author at www.heatherjean.org.

Published by Community Christian Ministries
P.O. Box 9754, Moscow, Idaho 83843
208.883.0997 | www.ccmbooks.org

Heather Jean Wilson Torosyan, *God's Master Plan for Women in Marriage*
Copyright © 2024 by Community Christian Ministries

Cover design by Samuel Dickison.
Interior design by Valerie Anne Bost.

All rights reserved. No part of this publication may be reproduced, stored in a retrieval system, or transmitted in any form by any means, electronic, mechanical, photocopy, recording, or otherwise, without prior permission of the copyright holder, except as provided by USA copyright law.

Unless otherwise stated, all Scripture quotations are from the New American Standard Bible®, Copyright © 1960, 1971, 1977, 1995 by The Lockman Foundation. Used by permission.

Scripture quotations marked KJV are from the King James Version, public domain.

ISBN: 978-1-882840-81-6

24 25 26 27 28 29 30 31 32 33   10 9 8 7 6 5 4 3 2 1

Contents

Foreword *1*
The Master Plan *3*
Companion *5*
Helper *9*
Submission *13*
Respect *15*
Communication *23*
More on Consideration, Respect & Submission *25*
How Do I Submit? *29*
Motherhood *35*
Titus 2: Called to Teach *37*
Gentleness *43*
Taking Offense *49*
Doing Good *53*

Foreword

I came to know Heather and her family in the spring of 1975 during my first year in Moscow, Idaho, where I had recently accepted the Lord as my savior. At the time, I was teaching Latin at the high school and the University of Idaho. We soon became fast friends, and from the start, I was aware that Heather was unique/remarkable—joy radiated from her.

She was great-hearted, caring, kind, friendly to all she met, particularly interested in reaching international students and their spouses, and most notably, she loved the Lord with her whole soul, mind, and strength. I observed these qualities in her while she was still quite young, only nineteen.

Reliant on God's grace, she played a role in the conversion of many to the Lord. Heather reached out to the rejected and unlovely from an early age and had a tremendous passion for sharing the gospel with internationals. This led her to Turkey as a missionary, where she met her husband Ararat.

Heather was blessed with godly parents, both excellent teachers, and she inherited their gift for teaching. Some years ago, she spoke at a women's retreat for her church in California on the role of Christian wives. The first portion of this small book was taken from that talk.

Heather's sudden departure to the Father's heavenly home in 2020 left an enormous hole in many hearts, including mine, but I rejoice that she left behind her wise, godly words from which we can learn. As you read, bear in mind that she did not just "talk the talk," but faithfully "walked the walk," and the fruit of her godly and faithful labor is evident in all those whom she touched in life. Lord willing, even more fruit will crop up from the insights she passed on in her writing!

Undoubtedly, the Lord welcomed home my dear friend with the words that all believers long to hear at their earthly life's end, "Well done, good and faithful servant! . . . . Come and share your master's happiness!" (Matt. 25:21).

I pray that all readers will be enriched and blessed by Heather's teaching in this volume.

MARNY LEMMEL
2024

The Master Plan

Much of what and how we think about ourselves is determined by our culture—by the time we live in now—by television, movies, and magazines, most of which are not only not Christian, and not neutral, either, but *anti*-Christian. But we are Christians, and, as Christians, we must think *biblically* about who we are, how we should behave, what we are doing here, and what our purpose is. Many people ask the questions "Who am I?" and "Why am I here?" and, more specifically, who are we as *women*, and why are we here. As Christian women, we must focus on these same questions in light of our faith.

We can look to our traditional culture (and yes, Americans do have one!) no matter where we are from, or we can look to modern culture for the answers. But the answers we need are not going to come from your culture or my culture, old culture or new culture.

We hear a lot about *traditional family values*, but tradition has nothing to do with the answers we are seeking. Tradition can be bad. Instead of traditional family values, we need *biblical family values*. If we want to know who we are and what we are for, we need to look to our Creator. He made us with a purpose. He has a plan. He is the master planner, and He has the answers. To define ourselves as women, and as Christian women, we need to ignore the teaching of our culture and look to the Scriptures for His answers.

Every woman will have different roles to play throughout the course of her life. All of us have been daughters. Many of us are sisters and wives, or sisters-in-law. I was a sister-in-law long before I was a wife. Many women are mothers or grandmothers. Some of us have not ever been married. However, Eve, the first woman, was created as a *wife*—not as a daughter, not as a sister, not as a mother.

Much of this book is geared toward wives, but the teaching in it applies to both married and unmarried women. All older women, called to teach the younger women, can share what they learn.

Companion

For the master plan, we look first at creation: "Then the Lord God said, 'It is not good for the man to be alone; I will make him a helper suitable for him'" (Gen. 2:18). Up to this point in creation, everything that God had created was good. He created the sea, and it was good, the stars, moon, fish, etc., and He deemed them good. Finally, He created man, but He didn't label man in the same way. While it almost seems as though He was about to say, "It is not good," there is a rider attached: "It is not good *for man to be alone.*" While Eve was created as a woman and a wife, she was primarily created to be a companion to Adam. If Adam simply needed somebody to boss around, he had all of creation for that. He was lord of creation, in charge over everything. That is not what Adam needed. Eve was created to be his *companion.*

What kind of companion are you going to be? You could be a pleasant companion, someone who is enjoyable to be around. Or you can be the kind of companion who is a torture to be around—like being stuck on a desert island with your worst enemy. Your enemy may technically be a companion, but you would prefer he was not there. Granted, there are many degrees between those two options, the torturous companion and the delightful one. There are certain days of the month when a wife is not a good companion and other times of less-than-good behavior.

Whether you are already married or planning to be married, I am assuming that you are committed to staying with your husband for life. Perhaps some have considered leaving, but not seriously. Billy Graham's wife Ruth was once asked if she had ever considered divorce. She responded, "Divorce, never. Murder, yes." We all know that sometimes we can get to that point with our husbands. We might never consider leaving them, but we might give them grief for as long as we are with them. We are committed to marriage. We must also be committed to being good and pleasant companions.

What could we do that would make us be *unpleasant* companions to our husbands? Nagging and criticizing top the list for many of us. We criticize our husband's leadership, his fathering, how much time he spends with the children, his lack of communication. We pick at him for not being a good provider (at least in our eyes), for being insufficiently spiritual, or for not picking up his dirty socks. On it goes. Any number of things can irritate us.

We love our husbands . . . but they need their weaknesses pointed out to them, right? While we might not be willing to say this out loud, we seem to believe, as our actions indicate, that God has given us the responsibility of showing our husbands what is wrong with them.

Do you think that your husband is not aware of what his problems are? I know a woman who, every time she got together with her sisters, told them that they were overweight and that they ate too much. Finally, I told her that she did not need to point out this problem to them every time she saw them. They already knew! This woman genuinely believed she was *helping* her sisters by constantly reminding them. I explained that she not only was not helping through her nagging, but was causing resistance to what she was wanting done. The more she nagged, the *less* likely they were to do anything about it. This is the way nagging almost *always* works. If you want someone to *not* do something, try nagging them about it.

Helper

The second reason God created woman was to be a helper. "It is not good for the man to be alone; I will make him a helper suitable for him" (Gen. 2:18).

Our role as wives is to be an *assistant* to our husbands for the work God has given them to do. We must understand that in the Master's plan the woman was never to be the leader. She was created to be the follower, the assistant, the suitable helper. *Suitable* means to fit. If someone goes to get clothes fitted, does the tailor fit the person to the suit or the suit to the person? The answer seems obvious—the suit is adjusted to the person, not the other way around. Likewise, because wives are to meant to be suitable to their husbands, we need to adapt to them.

Unmarried women should consider this design of God's in advance. While I was single, when I noticed a fellow, mentally I asked myself, "Would I want to submit to that guy?" Would I want to be a pleasant companion to him? Was I willing to have him as my leader? A woman should consider these things before she agrees to be someone's wife.

This flies in the face of what the world teaches. The world tries to pretend that marriage is a 50/50 proposition. However, you cannot have two *leaders* if you want anything to work. It might sound good in theory, but it simply won't work. A country cannot have two presidents; a ship does not have two captains; a car does not have two steering wheels. It sounds fair when marriage is called a 50/50 arrangement. Realistically, it does not and cannot work.

How can you be your husband's helper? The first things that come to mind might be activities like keeping the house clean and cooking. These are a good place to start. But how much are you involved in encouraging your husband's work or showing interest in what he does all day? We certainly appreciate them taking interest in what we do all day. *Take an interest* in your husband's work. As for me, I certainly know more about hydraulics than I ever thought possible!

You can also help your husband by meeting his sexual needs. You want him to be faithful to you in mind and body. Does he regularly hear excuses like, "Not tonight, dear," "I don't feel like it," or "I have a headache"? He shouldn't need to beg. On a sitcom, I once saw a fellow with a street woman, and he told her that if he wanted to beg for sex, he could simply go home. Those words were very revealing. Women want to be in control at home. There are many women out there in the world who are willing to be pleasant companions to your husband and willing to meet his sexual needs. You can be a helper to him by meeting them pleasantly yourself.

Even if we work outside the home, women are very home-oriented. We tend to want our husbands to be the same way—oriented towards the home and towards us. The problem is that while God created us to be oriented to our husbands, He did not create them for the same purpose. Do not let this cause disharmony in your relationship. Your husband's orientation is meant to be different from yours. This is not a fault in him; it is part of God's design in creation.

Submission

This brings us to a third and crucial job for wives. "But as the church is subject to Christ, so also the wives ought to be to their husbands in everything . . . . This mystery is great; but I am speaking with reference to Christ and the church" (Eph. 5:24, 32).

Paul specifically states that the relationship of husband and wife is a picture of Christ and the church. When we have an urge to put our husbands in their place, what are we saying about Christ? We are presenting the world with a faulty picture. That is exactly what the church appears to be doing now—attempting to have Christ submit to it rather than the other way around. Our marriage relationships should show the world how His bride, the church, submits to Christ. If we don't do it, it is not good.

Here's the problem: our husbands are not Christ. They don't love us like Christ loves us. Of course, our own submission is so *perfect*, right? No. It is easy to see other people's faults. I see that my husband doesn't love me as Christ loves the church. *Of course*, I myself am submitting lovingly, willfully, and respectfully . . . right? Always look to yourself to see what you can do there. Don't wait for your husband to do his part. "I'll do that when he does this." No—obey God on your own.

Neither gender is created holier or smarter than the other. Ephesians 5 is not talking about worth. Men and women are *both* modeling Christ and the church together. If anything, the husband's role (to model Christ) is more difficult than what wives are called to do.

Respect

Related to submission is the matter of respect. God has created people with the need to *give* respect and the need to *receive* it. Another word for respect is *honor*. In our relationship to God, we are to honor and respect Him. *Respect* does not mean having a warm fuzzy feeling. If I say that I love God, but I never do anything He tells me to do, I am not honoring or respecting Him.

In the Bible, we are told to respect our parents. The reason given for the command is that "He the Lord is God" (cf. Ex. 20:2). The reason we need to respect our parents is that God is God. Nowhere does the Bible say that we are to respect our parents because they are perfect. We are also told to honor and respect our elders, which it calls "the grey-headed ones."

Respecting God follows the respect and honor to your parents. John asks, "How can you love God when you hate your brother?"

(cf. 1 John 4:20). In the same way, how can you respect God when you don't respect the people in front of you? The two go hand in hand. The respect we show to people is a sign of the respect we have for God. As parents, do we want our children to respect us because we have an ego problem? No. We teach them to be respectful people, people who do not go against authority when they should not. Also, they will grow up knowing how to respect God. Respecting their parents teaches them to respect God.

In the first chapter of the book of Esther, Queen Vashti, wife of the King of Persia, was summoned to come show her beauty to all the princes of the land at a party. The men were "merry with drink." Vashti's response was, in modern terminology, "Are you kidding? I'm not going in there with a bunch of drunk men"—or whatever her reason, she said no. I must admit that I sympathize with her. I might have responded in the same way. However, did the king ask her to do something immoral, going before the princes to display her beauty? Was he asking her to commit adultery? Was he asking her to lie? We may safely assume that she was clothed. Perhaps we sympathize with Vashti because we cannot imagine complying if asked to do something similar. Despite our rush to sympathy, Scripture does not indicate that the king asked his wife to do something immoral.

Following Vashti's refusal, the king sought advice from his wise men. They immediately saw the implications of her disobedience. She had set a bad example. If the *queen* could ignore her husband, why couldn't any woman ignore her husband? The disobedience of the queen would cause havoc in homes all over the kingdom; women across Media and Persia would hold their husbands in contempt. Contempt is the opposite of respect. It is looking down your nose at someone. If the king did not act quickly, women across the kingdom would soon be showing disdain for their husbands.

Through the guidance of the king's advisors, Vashti lost her queenship, and Esther became queen. In this story, there was one king and two queens. Those two queens handled their husband very differently. How did Esther handle this man whom Vashti had disdained? Esther was very respectful of him. I believe that Esther succeeded in saving the Jews because she did things respectfully. We do not know Vashti's attitude. Perhaps she could have refused in such a way that the king would have accepted her choice not to appear. But the point is that men, even non-Christian men, understand that respect is important. To be embarrassed by their wives in front of others is mortifying.

We might be tempted to think that while non-Christian men want and demand such respect, Christian men should not care whether they are respected by their wives; they should be above needing respect. And because Christian wives think that, they disrespect their Christian husbands. It should be the opposite. Christian wives should be *more* respectful than non-Christian wives.

If a child is unloved, he starts asking for love, but he asks for it in ways that make him unlovely (by disobeying or acting out). This results in people loving him less, so he does it more. If you respect a man who is not acting respectable, it will not make him act *less* respectable. It will fill his need. He will demand respect *less*. He will act more respectable when he is given respect. When husbands are respected by their wives, they will not seek respect elsewhere.

All men (not just husbands) need this respect both in public and private. Women need respect as well, but they are more able to live with less of it than men are.

"'A son honors his father, and a servant his master. Then if I am a father, where is My honor? And if I am a master, where is My respect?' says the LORD of armies to you, the priests who despise My name! But you say, 'How have we despised Your name?' You are presenting defiled food upon My altar. But you say, 'How have we defiled You?' In that you say, 'The table of the LORD is to be despised'" (Mal. 1:6-7).

In this passage, God is addressing the priests who had asked how they were dishonoring the Lord. Have you ever heard a wife say, "I never disrespect my husband. How have I disrespected him?" They don't see how they do it. They are blind to it. One thing I suggest is to ask your husband, "Have I ever disrespected you?" He may tell you, "Well, there was this one time that I was so embarrassed, but I didn't want to say anything about it."

You might say that your husband doesn't mind how you talk about him because you were just joking. Let's assume this is true. Even if your husband knows you're joking, and you know you're joking, the people who hear you may not know, and consequently they might think less of him because of what you said.

Another temptation is that we sometimes feel that our own right to speak and express our views to and about our husbands is more important than obeying God's direct order.

In 1 Peter 2:17-18, God gives us a command to respect all people. "Honor all people, love the brotherhood, fear God, honor the king. Servants, be subject to your masters with all respect, not only to those who are good and gentle, but also to those who are harsh." The first command applies to everybody. We are to respect all people, love the brothers, fear God, honor the king. We must respect everybody and leave out nobody.

In verse 18, Peter tells slaves how to respect their masters. It is important to note that he did not say to only respect the good ones or the gentle ones. Peter tells servants to respect *unreasonable* masters. The same thing applies to wives. Of course, it's very easy to respect a husband who praises your cooking every night, or who regularly offers to take the family out to dinner at a nice restaurant to give you a break. It would be very easy to respect such a kind and considerate husband. If your husband is difficult or unreasonable, how can you be expected to respect him?

None of us is married to a perfect man. You might object here: you might say I don't understand because my husband is so good. But I am not the one telling wives to respect their husbands. God is giving the orders. We are to respect our husbands all the time, just like they are to love us all the time, not just when we are at our best.

Treating others with respect applies to everyone you have contact with. My dad often talked about respect. One time, my older brother asked him what he would do if he was walking down the street and ran across a drunk lying in the gutter. My dad said, "I would go up to him and say, 'Sir, can I help you?'" Not, "You lazy bum, get out of the gutter!" Use respectful words and a genuine attitude of respect to *everyone*. That means even the disagreeable people (even the telemarketers!).

What if you have a bad husband—one who is abusive or unfaithful? If this is the case, speak to him first. Don't go talk to all your friends about it. Don't complain about him to everyone. Talk to him first. Then speak to the elders at your church. When you are having a serious problem like this, the elders should be called in.

Ephesians 5:33 says that wives are to *see to it* that they respect their husbands. That means to make a point of it, to make it a priority.

Since God commands us to respect our husbands, we can infer that God sees that our husbands *need* respect. Therefore, we need to give it. A wife who doesn't respect her husband is in a bad way. Remember that our marriages are picturing the church's relationship with Christ. We respect our husbands the way the church respects Christ. We are not told to respect our husbands because they have an ego problem, and they want some puffing up. If they do have an ego problem, it is not our business. It is not our job to keep our husbands humble.

One of the reasons God tells wives to make a point of respecting their husbands is that we naturally have trouble doing it. We wouldn't do it if He didn't tell us to. In the same way, God tells husbands to love their wives because men have difficulty with *that*. Women don't. Women find it easy to love. When it comes to romance, a woman can love an idiot. However, she won't respect him.

How can someone respect such a man? For one thing, wives are commanded to respect the *man*, not his weaknesses. This does not mean condoning or approving of sin he is committing. You are not respecting the sin. You are respecting the man. Respecting a sinful man is not the same as respecting his sinful actions. His sin does not give you a loophole to get out of respecting him.

Back in the 1960s, my father spoke to a woman who had been married for about forty years, and the marriage was breaking up. My dad told her, "Think of something from the last forty years that you can respect your husband for."

She thought and thought and could not think of one thing. Finally, she said, "In the '30s, during the Great Depression, he always had food on the table; he always provided for us."

My dad said, "Go tell him. Open your mouth and tell him that you respect him for how he provided for your family."

She did it. Her opening her mouth and *verbalizing* her respect for him saved that marriage. Suddenly, after forty years of being put down, forty years of being nagged about why he didn't do this or that, forty years of being told everything that he wasn't doing right, he was given *respect* instead.

Many wives know the importance of encouraging their children. Don't forget that the men need it, too.

Communication

Marriage seminars love to focus on the need for good communication in marriage. There's just one problem: women *like* to communicate, and men do not.

Women tend to think all our marriage problems would be solved if only our husbands would tell us what they are thinking. If I were talking to men, I would encourage them to communicate more.

When our husbands don't talk, we tend to assume we know what they are thinking. These assumptions are typically negative. We build a dark, evil thought-castle on assumptions which probably have nothing to do with reality. These thoughts get us all bent out of shape, and we become unpleasant companions. And it's all for nothing, because we are *assuming*. My advice is don't assume. If you must insist on assuming something, then assume that *your assumptions are wrong*.

Again, Scripture does not say, "See to it that you keep your husband humble." It also does not say, "See to it that you communicate with your husband." We could object that if our husbands truly loved us as Christ loves the church, they would communicate more. That is something that could be addressed if I were writing to husbands. But this is about your responsibilities.

Not all communication is good. Yelling, screaming, and verbal abuse are communication. Such communication is to be avoided.

If we continually harp on our husbands' silence in response to our talking, we become nags. Nagging is unpleasant, and the Bible tells wives to be *pleasant* companions.

We want our husbands to talk to us—about the future, his plans for the house and his career, his concerns about the children, etc. Yet, as we talk to them, are we communicating our respect for them? If you want to communicate with your husband more, communicate *respect*. Instead of interrogating him ("Honey what do you think about this? What do you think about that? Tell me what you are thinking. What are you thinking?"), communicate your respect for him. Do you respect him but never tell him? *Tell him*. Go into detail about what you respect him for. Respect builds husbands up the way love builds wives up. Build your husband up by communicating your respect out loud.

More on Consideration, Respect & Submission

Respecting someone is not just saying, "Yes, Sir! No, Sir!, Yes, Sir!" It is *being considerate of them*. Consideration means thinking of the other person.

How do you know when you are not showing respect? Some clear examples include rolling your eyes when your husband asks you to do something; sighing; and complaining and/or criticizing (to him or to your friends, your mother, etc.). Those are showing disrespect.

Think about how we would treat an elderly person or a heavily pregnant woman who is getting on a crowded bus with no seats available. What would you do? You would immediately get up and offer your seat. You would *show consideration*, not have a "me first" attitude.

When we don't feel like we are getting what we need, we start grabbing for ourselves. This is a natural response, but it is not a godly one, and it is not effective, either. The best way to be treated well is to treat others well. The best defense is a good offense. Don't base your behavior toward your husband on a demand that you receive what you believe are your needs. Instead, keep showing respect, keep being considerate.

When you are very familiar with someone, you know all his weaknesses. This can make it more difficult to respect him. Knowing your husband's weaknesses does not mean you need to enlarge upon them. Don't focus on his weaknesses. Focus on respect and consideration. Giving your husband respect will help to strengthen him—just like you need to be loved when you are a mess and definitely not feeling lovely, he needs to be respected when he is weak. Husbands loving their wives makes the wives lovelier; and wives respecting their husbands makes their husbands more respectable. Respect is food to him.

If you have been a churchgoer for any amount of time, you have probably heard something about wives submitting to their husbands. *Submitting* means yielding control or power to another, surrendering, or deferring to someone else's judgment. Let me give you a secular example. In the navy, an officer on a ship may give his intelligent, expert opinion on something, but the captain of the ship makes the decision. The officer defers to the captain's judgment, whether it goes against his opinion or not.

Submission is not just for women. As Christians, we are to submit to God (James 4:7); we are to submit to the government and to those in authority over us (Rom. 13); we are to submit to the elders in our church (Heb. 13:17); and children are to submit to their parents. Christ submitted to God. All Christians are to do these things.

Submission is not an evil word. If people do not submit to the government, what happens to society? Anarchy. If children do not submit to their parents, or if wives do not submit to their husbands, what happens to the family? Chaos in the home.

Ephesians 5:22 says, "Wives, submit yourselves to your own husbands as you do to the Lord." An important thing to note here is that the Bible requires wives to submit to *their own husbands*. It does not say to submit to your favorite Christian teacher. You're not supposed to raise your children a particular way "because Dr. Dobson said so." You are to submit to your own husband, not to someone else's: not to the church elders, not to a Christian author you like, not to anyone but your own husband.

How Do I Submit?

The key to all of this is the *how*. Consider a servant and his boss. A good servant does serve his master, but ultimately, who is he serving? When he submits to his master, he is serving God. "Slaves, be obedient to those who are your masters according to the flesh, with fear and trembling, in the sincerity of your heart, *as to Christ*" (Eph. 6:5). Wives are to submit to their husbands the same way. "Wives, be subject to your own husbands, *as to the Lord*" (Eph. 5:22).

This makes submission so much easier. If I am doing something around the house that I don't like to do, like washing the dishes or cleaning the bathroom, I can do it *to the Lord*. If I do that task for the sake of anything but God, I might fall into difficulty with my attitude. Doing it to the Lord makes it possible for me to do it joyfully.

It is not good enough just to give lip service. Submission needs to come from the heart. Because of that, submitting gracefully can only be accomplished by doing it to the Lord. Instead of viewing our husbands as pigheaded fellows that we don't want to submit to, keep in mind that we are doing whatever they may ask of us as "to the Lord." Do it for Christ.

Of course, I'm assuming that your husband is not asking you to rob a bank or to perform some other illegal act. If that is the case, you certainly do not need to submit to him, and you may need to talk to the elders of your church. But the reason for refusing to submit to your husband in this instance is that you *do* need to submit to God, who says not to do those things.

However, most of the time when we balk at submitting, it is because the request is just not our cup of tea. We don't *want* to do it. It has nothing to do with morality or anything else. It may have to do with convenience or efficiency (this isn't the best way to do it), or with our personality (not something you're comfortable at doing), or with a disagreement (you think your husband is making the wrong choice in this decision—but not a sinful choice, like bank robbery). Nonetheless, we are to do it *as to the Lord*—joyfully.

The Bible does not tell women to submit to *men*. This point needs emphasis. "Wives, be subject to your husbands, as is fitting in the Lord" (Col. 3:18). Women are not under men in general. A woman is to submit to her father when she is young and unmarried, and then she is to submit to her husband once she is married. Women are not under the authority of just any man—only your own husband. In the church, of course, the entire congregation is to submit to the elders, but that is church government, not male-female submission.

Ephesians 6:5-7 gives us good instruction on how to be submissive. Paul was speaking here to slaves, but what he says applies whether we are submitting to husbands, or parents, or bosses. "Conduct yourselves with wisdom toward outsiders, making the most of the opportunity. Your speech must always be with grace, as though seasoned with salt, so that you will know how you should respond to each person."

This instruction in Ephesians is specifically for the workplace. If a woman is working at a job, she has to submit to whoever she is working for. Sometimes she may be asked to do something stupid—not wrong, but something she does not want to do. Ephesians says that in this situation we are to submit *in the sincerity of our hearts* and that our submission is not to be just eye service, done only when bosses are looking, or as people-pleasers (Eph. 5:22). Do it graciously. Do it with goodwill—willing good from our hearts, even when we don't think it's the best way or the right way.

When we submit as to Christ, we can submit *respectfully*. You could "submit" while rolling your eyes. That doesn't fly with God. We might still get the task done the way our husband wanted it, but it makes for unpleasantness in the home. God says we are to submit sincerely from the heart. He always looks at the heart. God is not as concerned with *what* we do, as with *how* we do it. Does God really care about which store we go to first? If we're out running errands together, and our husband wants to go to one store first, and we think it would be better to go to the other store first, does God really care which sequence is more efficient? I don't think so. He cares how we do our daily tasks, by which I mean that He cares that we do them graciously, pleasantly, lovingly, respectfully. There are a lot of things we might tend to think are important that God does not really care about—but He always cares about the *attitude* with which we do them.

It is easy when our husbands ask us to do something we want to do. When my husband recently suggested I take a break and go out to Black Angus for dinner with him, I didn't have any trouble "submitting" to his decision! Submission only becomes an issue when our husbands ask us to do something we don't want to do. We have to do it respectfully and graciously, and the best way to do that is to say, "This is for God." And it truly *is* for God, because God told us to do it. So if we do not do it, we are not only disrespecting our husbands, we are disrespecting God. Putting God in the picture makes submission much easier. Practice expressing respect to your husband and actively cultivate an *attitude* of submission in your day-to-day life. This will make the individual acts of submission which you may need to do from time to time so much easier.

When you recommend something to your husband, and he takes your advice, and it turns out wrong, *he* is responsible. He made the decision. He didn't have to take your advice, but he chose to do it. If he does not do what you say, and it turns out that he was wrong and you were right, the respectful thing is to *not* say, "I told you so." That is disrespectful. He knows what you told him; he knows that what he decided to do was wrong. Just let it go. Don't rub salt in the wound.

Again, a wife is to be a good companion, a pleasant companion, a respectful companion, a helper, an assistant, the second in command. Your marriage should reflect Christ and the church. Submit as the church does to Christ. Respect should be the attitude of our lives in general. Respect is not just for wives regarding their husbands. All believers should respect everyone. We are to do everything we do with respect, even sharing the gospel: "Sanctify Christ as Lord in your hearts, always being ready to make a defense to everyone who asks you to give an account for the hope that is in you, but *with gentleness and respect*" (1 Pet. 3:15).

One last note on respect: if you have a truly bad husband who is physically abusive or unfaithful, the respectful thing to do is to speak to him first. We are not to go off complaining about him to all our friends or even our mother. Talk to him first, and *then* speak to the elders. Talk to people who can be part of a solution.

Motherhood

Many wives are also mothers. From infanthood through their primary and secondary school years, until the kids go off to college or get married, the emphasis is on being a *nurturing* mother. Once you are a mother, you are always a mother, but the *mothering* we do lasts for a limited time. We are *married* till death do us part. We tend to think that motherhood is the greatest calling, but we need to remember that woman was created first as a *wife*. Motherhood came second.

Today, there is a great attack on motherhood and its importance. Should women have children? Should they stay at home with those children when they are young? The world says perhaps not. The world tells us that if a woman gets paid to babysit, perhaps owns a daycare center and watches other people's children, that is more honorable than staying at home with her own children because she is getting paid for it. The world says a paycheck is more fulfilling than raising children. The world's way of thinking is that something is only fulfilling when you get paid for it.

The Armenian culture I live in doesn't have this problem. They don't send their children to daycare; there are grandparents and other family members in the community to care for the children. My opinion is that our mothers raised us, and now it is our turn to *raise our own children*. Those of us who were young adults in the 1980s were part of what is called the "me generation." We had everything done for us, and now we want everyone to continue doing everything for us.

Instead, we need to think about how God created us. Scripture says that women are to be "workers at home" (Titus 2:5). Not much is said directly in the Scripture about women staying at home to raise their children. However, when Paul was writing to Timothy about the qualifications for a widow who was to receive support from the church, he says they should be those who have "a reputation for good works; and *if she has brought up children*, if she has shown hospitality to strangers, if she has washed the saints' feet, if she has assisted those in distress, and if she has devoted herself to every good work" (1 Tim. 5:10).

You will not find a verse in the Bible that says, "You must stay at home with your children." But Christian women are being attacked by the world on this subject. Being a "stay-at-home mom," our culture says, is somehow wrong. We are told that it is unfulfilling to stay at home. I want to encourage all women not to be taken in by this lie, because there is no more important work than the raising of children. Too many women today are realizing too late that the fulfillment they thought they could find in a career was hollow, and what they really want in life is a husband and children.

Titus 2: Called to Teach

"Older women likewise are to be reverent in their behavior, not malicious gossips nor enslaved to much wine, teaching what is good, so that they may encourage the young women to love their husbands, to love their children, to be sensible, pure, workers at home, kind, being subject to their own husbands, so that the word of God will not be dishonored" (Titus 2:3-5).

I highly recommend doing your own study on this passage. The passage is addressed to older women, but it applies to all Christian women. Let's dive into what we can learn from it. First, we are called to be *reverent in action*. Do you know what reverent means? It means *respectful*. Here again we see the importance of respect. Here the command to respect concerns our behavior in general, not just the behavior of wives toward their husbands. This rules out flippancy, mockery, and other negative behavior. Respect should characterize our actions.

Next, we are told not to be malicious gossips. Malice is *a desire to hurt*. That is what is at the heart of malicious gossip. "Well, we're gossiping, but it's okay. So-and-so is getting married (or whatever). We're just passing news around." That is not what is being addressed here, but rather the kind of talk that has claws in it. Whether we are willing to admit it or not, we want to hurt another person with the words we are saying. Christian women are not to do that. Rather, we are to be reverent/respectful in our speech about others.

We are not to be alcoholics. This is self-explanatory.

We are to teach what is good. This is one of the passages where the Bible says women are to teach. The people we are to teach are the younger women, and the first thing we are to teach them is to *love their husbands*. Wait, isn't the teaching to respect husbands? I have a good friend who is a scholar of classical Greek, so I asked her which type of love this passage is talking about. (Greek, the language of the New Testament, has three different words for love.) I guessed that it would be *agape*, which is unconditional love, the kind of love God has for us. She told me that it is not *agape*, and it is not *eros* (romantic love), but *philia*, friendship love. This goes back to woman being created to be a companion, a friend, to her husband. We are also told to *love our children* with this friendship love. I imagine that many would agree that sometimes we love our children, but we don't like them! They can be obnoxious and get under our skin. We are to love them the same way we are to love our husbands.

Older women are also to teach the younger women to be *sensible*. This means not panicking when things go wrong. One thing God does not need is for us to panic. What are we able to do when we panic? Nothing. Be sensible. Use the brain that God has given you. There is no need for panic. Remember that God is in control. Do you tend to be fearful? Ask God to take that away. He is faithful.

We are to teach women to be *pure*. This applies to thoughts as well as actions. Modesty is one important aspect of this. Women's fashions are getting worse and worse. If you are a slave to fashion or even moderately influenced by it, modesty is going to be a real issue. Don't swallow the latest fashions untested. Ask yourself, "What are the designers thinking? What are they advertising? What is the message this outfit sends (whether I mean it to be sending that or not)?" Consider what you are telling others with the clothing you put on your body.

Older women are to teach the younger ones to be *workers at home* and to *not be idle*. I have a friend who is a stay-at-home mom. One time, her husband asked her what she did all day while he was gone, thinking there couldn't be much there to keep her busy—so, one day, she just didn't do it. When he came home, the house was blitzed. There were piles of laundry on the couch, a mess everywhere, and no dinner ready. He asked, "What happened?" She said simply, "I didn't do it." She didn't do "what she did all day."

Next, we are to teach the younger women to be *kind*. Sometimes, I can be sarcastic with my children. Sarcasm can be funny, when everyone knows you're being sarcastic and understands. But sarcasm can also be deadly. It can be biting and hurtful. We are not to do that; we are to be kind.

Lastly, we are to teach women to be subject to their own husbands.

All that the older women are to teach the younger women is aiming at the same goal: "so that the word of God will not be dishonored." The objective is not that we can have the perfect family.

Our objective is *a good testimony to the world*. In everything we do, we should take care that the way we treat others, our behavior, our speech, our life is not dishonoring to the Word of God. We should be kind, loving, and respectful, so that the Word of God will not be dishonored.

This concludes the portion of the book taken from Heather's talk to wives. We hope it has been enlightening and encouraging to you. The following chapters are a selection of Heather's earlier writings on similar themes—gentleness, taking offense, and doing good. We pray their message will strengthen your walk with God and encourage you in living according to His will.

Gentleness

H ave you ever read a portion of Scripture for perhaps the hundredth time and had to ask yourself, "How have I never seen that before?" Recently, this happened to me while reading one of my favorite parts of Scripture. The way the verse jumped out and practically bit me on the nose was partly due to reading it in a different translation. Here it is: Philippians 4:5 says, "Let your *forbearing spirit* be known to all men." The NIV renders it, "Let your *gentleness* be evident to all."

Matthew 5:5 says, "Blessed are the *gentle*, for they shall inherit the earth." I would like to focus on the importance of gentleness in the believer's life. As Christians, we are up against a hostile world, and we need to be tough. We need to have thick skins. But sometimes we spend so much time developing thick skins that our *hearts* become hard, too. Or perhaps we leave the gentleness to those who are naturally gentle, and the toughness to those who aren't naturally gentle. We stay in the comfortable grooves of our personalities rather than developing the qualities that God requires of us.

Those of us who are naturally tough need to make sure our gentleness is evident to all. Our close friends might know how soft our hearts are. If someone gets to know us really well, they will find out about our soft heart. Well, that is not what this verse says should be the case. It says our gentleness should be evident, i.e., *obvious*, plain as a pikestaff. To whom should it be obvious? Our close friends? Our relatives? No—this quality should be evident to *everyone*.

If you say that your gentleness is really there, just deep down, I suggest taking a look to see if it is still there. The Word says, "For out of the overflow of the heart the mouth speaks" (Matt. 12:34). If the gentleness is there, it will come out. If it's not flowing out, something is wrong.

What is gentleness? The dictionary describes it as the quality of being kind, mild, quiet, not rough or severe, courteous, *tender*. In Ephesians, Paul enjoins us to be tenderhearted to each other. "Be kind and compassionate to one another, forgiving each other, just as in Christ God forgave you" (Eph. 4:32).

If we want to know what our gentleness should look like, it might help to think of how we see gentleness in normal life. We have all seen it (or been it) with newborns. Some of us may even be afraid to touch a newborn because we think we are not gentle enough. Or we remember how our mother tenderly took care of us when we were ill. On the emotional, spiritual, and mental planes, we can look after each other tenderly. As a gentle breeze is so refreshing on a hot day, so we can bring relief to each other with the revitalizing attitude of gentleness.

Look at it now from the reverse side. When is gentleness noticeably lacking in our lives? When are we not kind or courteous? Think of your attachment to your rights. Even a small thing like someone cutting ahead of you in line brings on the thought, "I'll give him a piece of my mind." That piece is not very gentle. Really, does it matter that much? My own temptation is to think of all sorts of witty (and cutting) remarks, which of course I'd never say. Unfortunately, God looks at the heart.

We love to champion justice, especially our own, but sometimes we are fighting real evil in the heavenlies made manifest on earth. Perhaps in fighting to stop the murder of the unborn we get pretty stroppy. We fight the feminist as if *she* is our enemy. Remember, the unsaved are just pawns of the enemy to work his evil. They are the devil's prisoners of war. "And a servant of the Lord must not quarrel but be gentle to all . . . in humility correcting those who are in opposition, if God perhaps will grant them repentance, so that they may know the truth, and that they may come to their senses and escape the snare of the devil, having been taken captive by him to do his will" (2 Tim. 2:24-26 NKJV). The Lord loves them, too—not just their unborn babies. There is always a need for balance—love the sinner and hate the sin. If we look at God's attitude toward sin (deserving of eternal death) and then look at the price He paid to redeem the sinner (you and me), we begin to get a glimmer of His perspective.

Another situation where Christians commonly fail to be gentle is when they encounter sin in the life of a fellow believer. If the sin is in our own life, we are apt to be gentle to a fault. We walk softly around the edges of our own failures. In our attempts to bring a straying brother or sister back to Christ, there may be times when we are required to be tough with our actions, but our hearts must always be gentle towards them. And that heart attitude should be obvious.

Do you like to argue theology? Friendly theological debates can quickly deteriorate into attacks on the other person's ability to think, read, use their grey matter, etc. Debates can be good, refreshing, and healthy if done in a spirit of gentleness and humility. However, sometimes the temptation to be witty at the other person's expense is pretty hard to resist. Look for a way of escape. Don't lose your perspective: remember that the person you are arguing with is more important than the argument.

As always, look to Jesus as your example. "Now I, Paul, myself urge you by the meekness and gentleness of Christ . . . " (2 Cor. 10:1). Paul urges the Corinthians by *the meekness and gentleness of Christ*. In Christ we see the perfect blend of toughness toward sin and gentleness toward the sinner. When Jesus was dealing with the woman caught in adultery, He was gentle. But he told her *in no uncertain terms* to leave that way of life. He was always gentle with those who knew they were sinners and were responding to Him. He is the Good Shepherd who goes after the one lost sheep. The rich young ruler, who did not respond to Jesus' call to follow Him, filled Jesus' heart with love. In every account of Jesus with sinners, that sense of gentle strength comes through. When dealing with those tangled up in their own self-esteem, He was harder in manner, but His heart was still soft towards them, as we see on the cross: "Father, forgive them; for they do not know what they are doing" (Luke 23:34).

Ephesians 4:1-2 tells us to "walk in a manner worthy of the calling with which you have been called, with all humility and gentleness, with patience, bearing with one another in love." Gentleness is not only for those who are naturally gentle; it is not a quality only necessary for mothers or people who work with children or the sick and aged. It is a requirement for all of us who are Christians. It is part of living a life worthy of our Lord.

As our Lord was gentle, so must we be.

Taking Offense

"Love is . . . not easily angered, it keeps no record of wrongs" (1 Cor. 13:4–5).

James tells us that if a man can control his tongue, he is well-nigh perfect, capable of controlling his whole body (James 3:2). The difficulty is that there are so many imperfect people who have not yet learned to bridle the tongue. In the meantime, people are being hurt right and left by what other people say.

It is not only the tongue that can hurt, but also the actions. So not only must all our friends and acquaintances bridle their tongues; they must likewise apply this know-how to their bodies.

For some reason, we put all responsibility on the offender rather than the offended. I have no intention of excusing an uncontrolled tongue. The tongue must be controlled. But until it is, do I have a right to be hurt? Must I remain susceptible to hurt feelings until everyone else is perfect? It seems to me the less efficient of two ways to achieve the same result.

We would like to have people be so nice to us all the time that there would never be an occasion for us to be hurt. Obviously, this is unrealistic, so what I am suggesting is that the offended toughen up.*

One way to do this is by looking at the example of Christ. "He was despised and forsaken of men, a man of sorrows, acquainted with grief, and like one from whom men hide their face. He was despised, and we did not esteem Him . . . . He was oppressed and He was afflicted, yet He did not open His mouth" (Is. 53:3, 9). Any of us in this same position would consider that we had every right to be hurt. If that's the way they are going to be, see if I'm ever going to 1) speak to them again, 2) be nice to them again, 3) forgive them, or 4) die for them. Yet if this had been our Lord's reaction, He would never have gone to the cross.

"Have this attitude in yourselves which was also in Christ Jesus who, although He existed in the form of God, did not regard equality with God a thing to be grasped, but emptied Himself, taking the form of a bond servant and being made in the likeness of men. And being found in appearance as a man, He humbled Himself by becoming obedient to the point of death, even death on a cross" (Phil. 2:5–8).

We should have a like mind to Christ in these four aspects:

---

* "Toughen up" does not mean to build a wall or some other defense mechanism to keep from getting hurt. That does not work; that only makes you become hard and calloused. It *does* mean to follow Jesus as an example, as in 1 Peter 2:21. Jesus stayed vulnerable. The best way to keep from getting hurt is to follow Jesus and stay vulnerable. That person stays soft. He does not become hardened. The best way to "toughen up" is to stay open and take it. It hurts less. —Jim Wilson

- Don't grasp onto your identity or your rights.
- Empty yourself.
- Be a servant.
- Be humble.

With such an attitude, we can also endure all sorts of crosses for the joy that awaits on the other side, thinking nothing of the shame attached (Heb. 12:2).

Normally those closest to us are the ones who can hurt us the most. A stranger has much less capacity for hurting us than a husband, wife, friend, brother, or sister. When wounded by someone close, we tell ourselves, "If he really loved me, he wouldn't say that." But analyzing this statement reveals whom we are really thinking about. Are we thinking about the lack of love in the other person and how he needs help? No, we are thinking how his lack of love affects us. In other words, we are conceited—we are thinking about self and how everyone else's action relates to us. A very favorite passage of mine on love is 1 Corinthians 13. It says love is "not self-seeking, it is not easily angered, it keeps no record of wrongs" (v. 5).

When we feel hurt, it is because there is no ready forgiveness in our hearts. Forgiveness, by nature, does not keep a record of wrongs. In Ephesians 4:32, a well-known but rarely practiced verse, Paul tells us to "be kind and compassionate to one another, forgiving each other, just as in Christ God forgave you." We must forgive as we have been forgiven. Remember 70 x 7. There is no limit to the command, and certainly none to the Lord's ability to forgive.

Considering that for every temptation the Lord provides a way of escape, there is no reason any of us should ever be hurt again.

That sounds like a tall order, I know, and many would say it is impossible. But it is my belief that if the Lord promised a way of escape, each time it will be there.

Doing Good

I once read an autobiography of an Armenian woman who survived the massacres of the 1890s. One of the points she made in her book was that young Armenian girls learned to keep house from their mothers, but learned to cook from their mothers-in-law. I can't say that I have had a lot of success with that. My mother-in-law makes great *manti*,* which I love to eat, but have never learned to make. The Armenian food I make is of a simpler variety. What is it that puts people off learning to make some of the tastier Armenian foods, leaving it to their grandmothers or the professionals? The answer is: a lot of work. It is not difficult, but time-consuming.

What inspires us to learn to make these foods? Usually, it is the reward of the joy set before us. We will be blessed in the end, as

---

* Small Turkish meat dumplings

will our family. When my mother-in-law makes *manti*, she makes enough for each of her seven children to take home and feed their families. She also usually has four or five of her daughters and one *hinami* (co-mother-in-law) helping her. What would happen if partway through the *manti* recipe she decided that she wasn't seeing any results, so gave it up? Would that make sense? Maybe she got through a little bit of dough, enough for one serving for one person in the family. How would that go over? The reason she makes these great dishes in great amounts is the reward of both sharing and eating them, and appreciation is pretty sure to follow.

There are many duties in our lives that are time-consuming and don't necessarily garner us appreciation when we do them, although we may hear about it if we don't do them. In this category are tasks like cleaning the bathroom, getting the laundry done, doing the grocery shopping, getting dinner on the table every night. There are also the things that we do for the church, or our kids' school, or our community.

Do we ever get tired of doing the same things? They are good things, needing to be done, but there is no tangible quick reward for this work like there is with *manti*.

2 Thessalonians 3:13 says, "But as for you, brethren, *do not grow weary of doing good*." The implication from this exhortation/command is that is quite possible to grow weary in doing good. In Galatians 6:9, Paul says, "Let us not lose heart [be discouraged] in doing good, for in due time we will reap if we do not grow weary. So then, let us do good to all people, and especially to those who are of the household of the faith." Paul uses an agricultural metaphor here: we will reap a harvest if we do not grow weary. A farmer must plow, plant, wait, *then* harvest. The time to reap does not happen

overnight. If a farmer walks away halfway through the process, he will not be able to reap anything. So, having told the Galatians that they will reap a harvest if they persevere, Paul then tells them to go out and do good to all people, especially Christians. Living the Christian life is not a matter of just biting the bullet and getting through; there is going to be a reward, a blessing. So let's go out and do more good to more people.

But we are discouraged, we have lost heart, we are weary. 2 Corinthians 3:18-4:1 tells us, "But we all, with unveiled face, beholding as in a mirror the glory of the Lord, are being transformed into the same image from glory to glory, just as from the Lord, the Spirit. Therefore, since we have this ministry, as we received mercy, we do not lose heart." Paul tells us how these Christians did not lose heart. *They received mercy.* If you look in the early part of the quote, what had these people been doing? They had been beholding the glory of the Lord and were being transformed from glory to glory. *They received mercy.* If we look ahead "to the glory set before us," we can continue our work. Look to Christ. Look to Him for strength. Realize the value of what we are doing in our homes and in our day-to-day lives as Christian women; it is the Lord's work, and the results are His.

www.ingramcontent.com/pod-product-compliance
Lightning Source LLC
Chambersburg PA
CBHW072107110526
44590CB00018B/3350